Jake's Shadow

Chris Powling

Illustrated by Scoular Anderson

OXFORD
UNIVERSITY PRESS

Chapter 1
An extra-special shadow

Jake's shadow was messing around again. It poked out its tongue. It waggled its ears. It picked its nose ... then shook itself all over as if it had a fit of the giggles. 'Will you stop that stuff?' said Jake wearily. 'You're just a shadow, right? You're supposed to copy everything I do, not add bits and pieces of your own.'

His shadow shook even harder. Jake decided he'd had enough. 'OK, Shadow,' he said. 'You asked for it. I'm off to tell Mum.'

Mum was out in the garden hanging up washing. Jake's baby sister, Polly, was asleep in her buggy close by. Behind them, on the garden wall, was a lollopy old ginger tomcat. 'Scram, cat!' said Mum sharply. 'Babies and cats don't mix!'

'But Mum,' Jake protested. 'It's only the Mogster. He's been hanging around for years.'

'Well, from now on he can hang around somewhere else. He could give Polly a really nasty scratch. He might even stop her breathing if he sat on top of her!'

Mum shuddered as she shooed the Mogster away. 'That's better,' she said. 'Your little sister will be safe now. What is it you want, Jake?'

'Mum, we need to talk,' Jake sighed.

'What about?'

'My shadow.'

'Your shadow?'

Jake took a deep breath and told her the whole story. When he finished, he saw Mum wasn't impressed. 'Messing around?' she said. 'How can a shadow mess around on its own, Jake? A shadow copies whatever you do. It doesn't mess around by itself.'

'My shadow does,' said Jake.

Mum looked over her shoulder at the garden wall. She saw her own shadow. She saw the shadow of the buggy with Polly dozing inside it. And she saw Jake's shadow, so spiky-haired and Jake-shaped it couldn't have been anyone else.

'Go on,' Mum prompted. 'Let's see this shadow of yours messing around.'

'But it might be rude, Mum,' Jake warned.

'It'd be a brave shadow!' said Mum, folding her arms.

Of course, Jake needn't have worried. For the first time in ages, his shadow was on its best behaviour. In fact, just as a shadow should, it copied Jake exactly by doing nothing at all.

Mum lifted an eyebrow. 'Is that it?' she asked.

'Mum, it's trying to trick you by not messing around. Once you're not watching, it'll start again.'

'Not for long, Jake. See those clouds over there? They'll cover the sun in a moment and all these shadows will vanish, including yours. You only get a shadow if something blocks out the light. If there's no light ... well, there's no shadow.'

'Ah,' said Jake. 'That's another thing ... '

Mum was beginning to get cross. 'Don't tell me, Jake,' she snapped. 'Is this shadow of yours so extra-special that you can still see it even when the sun goes in?'

'That's right,' said Jake in surprise. 'How did you know what I was going to say?'

'I guessed,' said Mum dryly.

Jake saw she wasn't listening any more. She thought he was playing some kind of game. Already she'd gone back to fussing with Polly in her buggy and so had the Mum-like shadow

on the garden wall. Meanwhile, his own shadow
hadn't moved.

Or had it?

Jake peered at it a little more closely. Was it – very, very slyly – poking out its tongue again?

If so, it was making a big mistake. Jake wasn't at all the kind of kid who was scared of his own shadow. Besides, his mum wasn't the only grown-up he could ask. Maybe his dad would help him. There had to be someone in the house who knew how to deal with a mad shadow.

Chapter 2
Under attack!

Dad was preparing what he called a Summer
Bank Holiday Supper. This seemed to mean
using every pot and pan in the house – not to
mention every knife, fork, ladle, spoon, sieve and
spatula he could lay his hands on. The clutter all
round him looked like an explosion of cooking
kit waiting for some kind of rescue squad to
arrive. 'Your shadow, Jake?' he said, distractedly.
'Can't you can see how busy I am right now? Tell
me about it later on, OK?'

'But it's come alive, Dad!'

'Alive?' Dad straightened up. 'Jake, you don't seem your normal self. All these strange ideas … it's not the baby, is it? Is Polly getting to you a bit?'

'No,' said Jake tightly. 'She isn't.'

He slammed the kitchen door behind him as hard as he could. Outside in the hallway, he was surrounded by shadows. They spilled out of the picture frames. They sloped away from the banisters. They lurked so snugly in every nook and cranny that Jake couldn't tell if he was looking at a nook, a cranny or a shadow.

But where was *his* shadow?

Ah, yes. It stood waiting on the doormat. Jake goggled at it in horror. 'How come we're so far apart, Shadow?' he gasped. 'Shouldn't some bit of us be linked together?'

Of course, his shadow didn't answer. Instead, it crooked a finger and beckoned Jake to follow it.

A shadow that wants you to follow it? Jake

was so astonished, that's exactly what he did –
down the garden path, through the front gate
and out into the street. Mr Snoddy, the retired
soldier who lived next door, spotted him at once.
'Hello, Jake!' he boomed. 'Good to see you up

and about. I was on duty myself at the crack of dawn. Been giving the garden a spit and polish!'

'It looks really nice,' Jake said.

Mr Snoddy had the neatest garden Jake had ever seen. Every blade of grass seemed to be standing to attention. Every flower looked in mid-salute. Even the pebbles along the garden path had a ready-for-inspection look. Jake half expected a bugle call at any moment to announce some sort of parade.

No ... not a bugle call; the sound Jake heard next was more like the buzz of an electric motor.

Mr Snoddy swung round in surprise. 'Is that my lawnmower?' he exclaimed. 'It's computerized, you know. Just a tickle on one of its sensors and it does the job pretty much by itself. Good grief! It *is* doing the job by itself!'

'Er ... not quite by itself,' Jake said.

Behind the long, stretched-out shadow of Mr Snoddy's lawnmower, Jake had seen another

shadow – a shadow with spiky hair, a Jake-like shape and fingers already in mid-tickle! By now the lawnmower was roaring at full throttle. Suddenly, it plunged across Mr Snoddy's garden like a small, mechanical dragon out on the rampage. 'As you were, lawnmower!' barked Mr Snoddy in alarm. 'As you were!'

Too late.

It was as if the lightest possible fingertip – say, the shadow of a fingertip – had tripped all the lawnmower's sensors at once. First, it shaved the grass so closely that only bumpy stubble was left. Then, it swooped along the flower-beds snipping off every single bloom. Finally, it skimmed over the pebbles on the garden path. The lawnmower blades spat them in every direction like a hail of bullets. 'Take cover, Jake!' Mr Snoddy yelled. 'Throw yourself flat on the ground!'

Jake only just beat Mr Snoddy to it. The storm of stones only went on for a minute or so, but it was the longest sixty seconds of Jake's life. When the last rattle and ping had died away, he got slowly to his feet. So did Mr Snoddy – even more slowly. His eyes were fixed on the lawnmower lying still amongst the wreckage. 'Don't go near it, Jake,' he warned. 'This could be a trick. It may want to lure us out in the open so it can launch another attack.'

'I don't think so, Mr Snoddy,' Jake swallowed.

'How can you be so sure, lad?'

'Because it wasn't the lawnmower's fault. It was all down to my shadow fiddling with the sensors. I'm really sorry about your garden, Mr Snoddy. My shadow was definitely to blame!'

'Your shadow?'

'Didn't you see? It was really scary.'

'You're saying the culprit was your shadow, Jake?'

'Well, yes ... '

Jake's voice trailed away. There, down by his feet again, lay his shadow – all innocent and inky-black. 'Oh,' said Jake faintly. 'You've decided to come back to me, have you?'

'Come back to you?' spluttered Mr Snoddy. 'Are you telling me my garden has been vandalized by a shadow, Jake?'

'Mr Snoddy, please listen ... '

But the old soldier had heard enough of Jake's stories. With a smart about-turn, he tilted his head at a military angle and marched left-right,

left-right, left-right, straight for his house. Jake
let out a wail of dismay. 'That's great, Shadow!
Really great! Now I'm in big trouble!'

Not that this bothered his shadow. It did its

own smart about-turn, tilted its own head at a military angle and marched itself along the street – left-right, left-right, left-right, as if it knew all along that Jake was sure to chase it.

Chapter 3
Horsing around

It isn't easy chasing a shadow, especially if you live on the very edge of a city where the pavement stops and open country begins.

'Slow down, Shadow!' puffed Jake. 'I can't keep up with you!'

His shadow marched faster than ever. It flitted in and out of the sunlight, down a narrow lane and across a paddock, where Jake saw a huge stone horse trough. 'Just what I need,' he panted. 'Something to cool me down ...'

Jake bent over the trough, scooped up some water and splashed it over his face. It wasn't especially cold, not on a sunny day like this, but at least it washed off the hot, sticky sweat which had been running into his eyes. 'Fantastic!' Jake exclaimed.

'What on earth are you doing, young man?' came a lofty, piercing voice behind him.

Jake knew exactly who had spoken. It was Miss Saddlesaw, who ran the City Stables at the other end of his street. Miss Saddlesaw loved every living creature on earth ... provided it was a horse. In her view, if it wasn't a horse, it was a waste of space.

Smiling as politely as he could, Jake turned to face her. As usual, Miss Saddlesaw was wearing riding boots, riding breeches and a smart riding hat. Even her hair, hanging down at the back, was plaited like a horse's tail. She was mounted on a stringy-looking horse with a floppy mane and soft, sleepy eyes but Miss Saddlesaw patted its neck as if it were a thoroughbred. 'My dear old Sholto needs a drink,' she intoned. 'That's if there's any water left.'

'There's plenty, Miss Saddlesaw.'

'I should certainly hope so. Also, I hope it's still clean and fresh after you've been dabbling in it. You're Jake, aren't you? From the last house in the street, where they've got a little baby?'

'That's right, Miss.'

'Do you have a bathroom at home, Jake?'

'Yes ... '

'Well, kindly use it in future. And kindly leave troughs like this to the wonderful creatures they were built for.'

'But Miss ... '

Jake lifted a trembling finger. He was pointing beyond Sholto and Miss Saddlesaw to something dark, flat and eerie that was slinking over the grass towards them. 'Watch out!' Jake gulped. 'My shadow is just behind you!'

'Your shadow?'

'It's creeping up
on you, Miss!'

'Don't be
ridiculous, Jake. It's just
a cloud, I expect – '

This was as far as Miss
Saddlesaw got. Jake's shadow
was slithering through Sholto's
legs – except it wasn't Jake's
shadow now. When it popped up
under the old horse's nose, it had
taken the shape of a sleek, fully-grown
fox which twiddled its whiskers cheekily.

The horse reacted at once.

With a snort of fury, it shook its mane, dipped its head and kicked up both its back legs. Even a rider as good as Miss Saddlesaw was taken by surprise. She catapulted over Sholto's head, turned head over heels in the air, and belly-flopped into the horse trough with the sort of plonking, echoing splash you could have heard as far away as the city centre, never mind the end of the street. 'Aaagh!' she shrieked.

'Sorry, Miss!' Jake yelled. 'Gotta go!'

Nobody could blame him for that.

You see, his shadow – now spiky-haired and Jake-shaped again – was already sprinting lickety-split towards the Summer Bank Holiday Fun Fair it had noticed in the next field.

Chapter 4
The not-so-fun fair

Like most kids, Jake loved a fun fair. Soon he was gawping at the big wheel, the dodgems, the octopus ... with no sign of his shadow anywhere. 'I wish I'd brought some money,' he sighed.

Jake peered enviously at a little kid on the bouncy castle. She was jumping up and down so fast, it must have been hard for her shadow to keep up with her. Bounce-bounce-bounce it went ... its spiky hair standing out sharply against the castle's rubber wall.

Its spiky hair?

How come the little kid's hair was long and curly while her shadow's hair was spiky?

'Is that you, Shadow?' Jake gasped. 'Are you pretending you belong to other kids now?'

That's exactly what Jake's shadow was doing. If it fancied any of the rides, it nudged up to somebody who'd just bought a ticket. If they had a shadow already, who cared? Jake's shadow simply bundled it out of the way. Jake was horrified when he saw this. He'd better grab the shadow at once – before anyone noticed.

But how do you grab a shadow? Already it was drifting towards the ghost train. 'The ghost train?' Jake snorted. 'Ghost trains are useless. They couldn't even scare a baby like Polly.'

Silly Jake – he should have known his shadow better.

Quick as a blink, it slipped into the last carriage. There was just enough time for Jake to clamber after it as the man in charge let out a howl of fury. 'That kid hasn't got a ticket!'

'Sorry, mister!' Jake waved helplessly. The ghost train was gathering speed. Clanking and rattling, it lurched round a corner, into a tunnel, then plunged into darkness. There was a flicker of half-hearted lightning, a feeble wolfish howl and the rearing up of a dummy skeleton behind a cardboard gravestone.

'See what I mean?' scoffed Jake. 'Ghost trains are really pathetic!'

And so it was ... until his shadow went into action.

'What's that?' exclaimed a girl in the second-to-last carriage.

'What's what?' asked her boyfriend.

'That,' the girl pointed. 'Can't you see? It looks like the shadow of a vampire. Yuck! It's slurping away at my neck now. I think it wants to suck my blood!'

'So give it a slap!'

'That's what I'm trying to do. It's like slapping empty air. Eek! There it goes again – I'm being nibbled by Dracula's shadow!'

'Dracula's shadow?'

'Yes, Dracula's shadow!' the girl screamed.

Maybe it was the name that did it. Soon it was being passed from carriage to carriage as a joke. After all, what would a famous vampire be doing on a ratty old ghost train like this? But the laughter didn't last long. Jake's shadow saw to that. Now it tickled with shadowy fingers. Now it planted a shadowy kiss. Now it shadow-pinched and shadow-tweaked and shadow-prodded, each with a shadowy hint that something much worse was on its way. It swirled from one end of the train to the other like a nightmare come to life.

'Stop it, Shadow!' Jake begged.

But the shadow was having too much fun. By the train's third circuit of the track, everyone on board – apart from the spiky-haired boy in the last carriage – was in a shuddering, goose-pimply panic from the sheer creepiness of the bat-like shape ducking and diving all around them.

Not a moment too soon, the ghost train slowed and came to a stop. Instantly, every carriage door was flung open by the passengers inside. 'There's a vampire on the train!' they screamed. 'It's been trying to suck our blood!'

'A vampire?' exclaimed the man in charge. 'What a load of rubbish! I've been running this ghost train for years and this is the first I've heard of any vampire.'

'It's only my shadow,' Jake piped up. 'Honestly, it's pretending to be Dracula just to scare people.'

But who was listening by then? Besides, his shadow had already vanished into the crowd.

'OK, Shadow,' Jake muttered to himself. 'You're on your own. I'm going home, all right? Someone's bound to tell the ghost train man where I live. After Mr Snoddy and Miss Saddlesaw have had their say, that'll make three complaints in a row – all on the same day. Mum and Dad will have a meltdown. They'll probably ground me forever!'

Chapter 5
A wake-up call

It wasn't quite a meltdown – more like a big freeze, really. Polly was having yet another nap and Mum and Dad didn't want to wake her so they sent Jake straight to bed without any supper – the so-called Summer Bank Holiday Supper that Dad had been fiddling with all day. 'We'll talk about this tomorrow, Jake,' he said darkly.

'You bet we will,' Mum added.

Hours later, they still sounded cross when they came upstairs themselves. 'Sleep tight, Jake,' they both called out as they passed his bedroom door. No goodnight kiss for him, he noticed. Polly got lots of them, though. They fussed about in her room for nearly eleven minutes while they changed her nappy. Actually, it was ten minutes and forty-nine seconds, to be precise. Jake happened to be looking at his mobile at the time so he knew this for a fact.

Now he couldn't sleep. He tried lying on his front. He tried lying on his back. He tried lying on his left side. He tried lying on his right. Whichever position he took, it just didn't seem to work.

Was it the moonlight keeping him awake? The moon was so full and the sky was so clear that Jake's room was awash with silver, even though the curtains were shut tight. 'This is amazing,' he yawned. 'It's just like broad daylight. No, that's not right. More like broad nightlight, I suppose.'

In broad nightlight, every object in a room seems to melt into its own shadow. For instance, did the wardrobe in the corner cast a shadow? Or did the shadow in the corner cast a wardrobe?

Suddenly ...

'Jake!' said a dry, dusty voice.

'What?'

'You heard me.'

Slowly, Jake sat up. He rubbed his eyes with both hands. This made no difference at all to what he saw in front of him. There, at the end of his bed, was a dark, Jake-like shape topped off with spiky, Jake-like hair. Jake shrank back. He pulled the duvet up to his nose and peeped

nervously over the top of it. 'Are ... are you my shadow?' he whispered.

'Who else?'

'But you've just spoken to me – in your very own voice! Everybody knows a shadow can't talk!'

Jake's shadow gave a laugh as thin as a cobweb.

'Then everybody needs a wake-up call,' it said. 'I can talk like you, walk like you, look like you and think like you. What's more, Jake, I can do a whole heap of things you'd never dream of doing.'

'Yeah,' said Jake, ruefully. 'I've already seen that. How come you don't behave like a normal shadow?'

'Because I'm not a normal shadow. You should've worked that out for yourself with all the clues I've given you.'

Jake felt more uneasy than ever. Here he was, cooped up in his bedroom, with a shadow that wasn't a bit like himself. Well, not really. The trouble was, deep down he felt a tingle of excitement. How many other kids in the world have a shadow that isn't normal? Cautiously, he lowered the duvet. 'So why are you talking to me now?' he asked.

'I've had a summons, Jake.'

'A summons?'

'You know what a summons is?'

'It's a kind of invitation, isn't it? Except you're not allowed to say "no" to it. A summons is sort of compulsory.'

'Exactly,' his shadow said.

'So who sent you this summons?'

'Can't you guess, Jake?' said his shadow, smugly. 'It came from the boss, who else?'

'Er ... which boss is that?'

'The Shadow Boss, of course!'

Jake stared at his shadow, blankly. The truth was, he'd never heard of the Shadow Boss, but it didn't seem polite to say so. 'That's terrific, Shadow!' he said. 'What an honour! Er ... why has the Shadow Boss summoned you, I wonder?'

'To give me a medal, I expect.'

'A medal?'

'Solid gold, probably.'

'A solid gold medal from the Shadow Boss? Shadow, that's great! What's he giving you the medal for?'

'Bravery is my guess.'

'Bravery?'

'Jake, stop being so dim! Think of all the other shadows you've come across – the normal shadows. What's the only thing they ever do? They copy, that's what. If you stand up, they stand up. If you give a wave, they give a wave. If you start scratching, they start scratching. It's always the same – copy, copy, copy. Shadows are nothing but a bunch of copycats. Well, I'm not as boring as they are!'

'You certainly aren't,' said Jake.

His shadow gave a modest toss of its head. It lifted its hand, breathed on its knuckles and rubbed its chest in a polishing kind of way. 'That's why I deserve a solid gold medal, Jake. I'll wear it forever, twenty-four seven, to show how different I am.'

'If you say so, Shadow,' Jake said.

He almost smiled with relief knowing his shadow would be leaving at any moment. In fact, he was surprised it hadn't left already.

'Shouldn't you be getting a move on?' he asked. 'A summons is a summons, after all. You mustn't keep someone as important as the Shadow Boss waiting – especially if he's giving you a solid gold medal for bravery. I'm really going to miss you while you're away.'

'No, you won't, Jake.'

'Won't I?'

His shadow gave the same thin, cobwebby laugh Jake had heard before. 'You won't miss me a bit,' he said. 'You see, you'll be coming with me. *Your* name is on the summons, too.'

Chapter 6
The Shadow Boss

It was the oddest trip Jake ever took – not that
he saw very much of it. You can't while you're
clinging to your own shadow. Jake felt wrapped
from top to toe in a wafer-thin cut-out of
himself, like a snake that's shedding its skin. 'Er
… where are we going, Shadow?' he asked.

'To the Shadow Zone, of course. That's where
the Shadow Boss lives. It's where shadows go
when they're off-duty. We don't just disappear,
you know. Once the sun comes out again or
someone switches on a light, we must get back to
work instantly.'

'Like a den for shadows, you mean?'

'A den, a shelter, a haven – whatever you want
to call it. It's the place where we please ourselves,
Jake. There's no copying in the Shadow Zone. A
shadow can do as it likes.'

'So how soon will we get there?'

'We're already there.'

'Oh ...'

Suddenly, all Jake could see were shadows doing as they liked. They fluttered and danced around him like a whirl of flat black leaves shed from a giant beanstalk. He saw a shadow tree do a handstand. He saw a shadow skyscraper shrink itself almost to nothing, as if it fancied being a bungalow for a while. He saw ugly shadows turn pretty, skinny shadows expand and scruffy shadows smarten up.

His own shadow paid no attention at all. It scooted through the silvery darkness without glancing right or left. They turned a shadowy corner, ducked under a shadowy arch and pushed open a shadowy door. 'This is it, Jake,' his shadow announced. 'This is the biggest moment of my life! Get ready to meet the Shadow Boss!'

Jake heard the door swish shut behind him. Somehow, now they were indoors, the Shadow Zone seemed more shadowy than ever. There was no furniture – just shadow furniture. No carpet – just shadow carpet. No books or flowers or pictures – just shadow books and shadow flowers and shadow pictures. It was as if everything real had vanished ... and left only its shadow behind.

'This is creepy!' Jake exclaimed.

'Creepy?'

Jake gave a jump of fright. By now he was used to shadowy voices. This voice was much more than dry and dusty, though. It was so deep and dark and dreadful it sounded like a thunder-clap folded flat. 'For us, this is *comfy,* not creepy, Jake,' the voice continued.

Somewhere in the gloom, Jake sensed a huge, dim figure. But where was the Shadow Boss, exactly? It seemed to surround him and loom over him all at once. 'I'm glad you finally got here,' it rumbled.

'So am I,' Jake's shadow declared. 'This solid gold medal of mine has been a long time coming!'

'A solid gold medal?'

'For bravery, yes. Isn't that why you sent the summons, Boss? So you can present me with a solid gold ...'

Jake heard his shadow's voice trail away. The room had gone suddenly quiet. It was a strange, shadowy quiet. He heard the shadowy tick of a clock, the shadowy creak of a floorboard, the shadowy flap of a curtain at a shadowy window. Then the low growl of the Shadow Boss smothered everything. 'Are you serious, young shadow-me-lad?' it hissed. 'You really think you're here for a medal?'

'Why not?'

'After all your showing off?'

'My showing off?'

'How else can you describe your antics?'

'My ... my antics?'

The Shadow Boss gave a nod so vast and so awesome that the whole room seemed to nod along with it. 'I've never known a patch of black like you,' it rumbled. 'Not in all the days I've been cast. You're a disgrace to the idea of Shadowhood!'

Jake's shadow reeled back in shock. 'Me?'

'Yes, you. A shadow's duty is to follow. That's what it's for. It may be short at noon. It may be tall at dawn and dusk. It may disappear altogether when the conditions aren't right. Except for here in the Shadow Zone, it never ever takes the lead.'

'Look, I only wanted – '

'Oh, I know what you wanted. Believe me, you're not the first and you certainly won't be the last. Every so often – once in a lifetime, say – some jack-the-shadow comes along with a smirk on his lips and a heart full of tomfoolery. But you're far and away the worst of them. It's a wonder I haven't snuffed you out already.'

'Snuffed me out?'

'Like a candle – with one flick of my fingers.'

'No!' wailed Jake's shadow. 'No, Boss! There must be something I can do to put things right.'

'As a shadow? Not a thing. A shadow is born and bred to copy, remember. It's never the one in charge. So you're helpless as well as hopeless. I might as well snuff you out right now!'

Jake took a deep breath. 'Er ... I've just had an idea, Mr Shadow Boss. Why don't we change places?'

'Change places?'

'Let me and my shadow swap over. He becomes me and I become him for a while. That way, I can do all the copying while he puts right all the things he's done wrong – and we haven't broken any rules. When we've finished, you can swap us back to being ourselves again. Could you fix that, Mr Shadow Boss?'

For a moment there was silence. It was as if a big, shadowy brain was thinking things over. When the Shadow Boss spoke again, its voice was as cold and crushing as an avalanche of snow. 'Nothing simpler, Jake. It's a brilliant idea. The question is ... why would you trust a flashy little blot of darkness like this one?'

'Because he's *my* flashy little blot of darkness,' Jake sighed. 'And I don't want to lose him.'

'Fair enough ... '

'Fair enough?' echoed Jake's shadow. 'What's fair about it? Nobody's bothered to ask my opinion, I notice. I don't like the sound of this at all. I don't have to agree, do I?'

'Certainly not,' said the Shadow Boss. 'But let me remind you what happens if you don't.'

All at once, an enormous, shadowy hand hovered in the murky gloom above them like a thunderbolt about to fall. It made a candle-snuffing movement in the air. Jake's shadow gave a shriek of terror. 'It's a deal, Boss!' it yelped.

'Good,' growled the Shadow Boss. 'I'm glad we've got that sorted. The swap will begin tomorrow at sunrise. Jake, you'll wake up as your shadow. Shadow, you'll wake up as Jake. Remember, payback time is never easy. I want medal-winning behaviour from both of you.'

Jake's shadow stiffened. 'Medal-winning behaviour?' it exclaimed. 'You mean there's a chance I might still get one?'

Jake rolled his eyes in despair.

The Shadow Boss gave a low, long-suffering groan. 'Don't hold your breath,' it said.

Chapter 7
The Fake Jake

When the sun came up the next morning, Jake found he was a copycat – a flat, black copycat and as thin as a wafer. His shadow – the Fake Jake – was the one in charge now. Fake Jake pushed back the duvet. Fake Jake reached for a dressing gown. Fake Jake bustled into the bathroom next door. 'Come on,' he called back, cheerily. 'A proper shadow doesn't lag behind, you know. We must do things exactly together. That's what the Shadow Boss told us. It's a bit like synchronized swimming!'

To Jake's surprise, he soon got the hang of it himself.

What came next was a synchronized shower, synchronized teeth cleaning and synchronized going to the loo. By the time they got round to synchronized dressing back in the bedroom, Jake was as nippy as any shadow can be. Mind you, it did feel a bit peculiar. *It's like being a coat of paint*, he decided. *A coat of paint on the move. You sort of spread yourself as you go along.*

Something else felt peculiar, too. For the first time in his life he could see himself as others saw him. *Except it isn't me at all*, Jake frowned. *It's my shadow standing in for me – though nobody could possibly tell the difference.* That's what he hoped, anyway.

Dad looked up from his cornflakes the instant Fake Jake and his shadow came into the room. 'And how are you this morning?' he asked dryly. 'In a better mood, I hope.'

'I'm really sorry about yesterday, Dad.'

Fake Jake had pitched his voice just right. Slowly, Dad lowered his spoon. He glanced across the kitchen where Mum was feeding Polly. 'Go on then,' she said coldly.

'I want to put things right if I can, Mum. I'll start with the man at the fun fair, go on to Miss Saddlesaw's, then visit Mr Snoddy. I'll do any job they like, to make up for messing about.'

Dad gave a doubtful shake of his head. 'So where does this precious shadow of yours fit in?'

'My shadow?' said Fake Jake.

'It's right there beside you, Jake. According to you, it was responsible for everything. Not your fault at all, you said. So what's changed since then, may I ask?'

Fake Jake said nothing. After all, how could he admit he had changed places with the real Jake? That would ruin the whole plan. Luckily, at that very moment, there came a sudden ear-splitting

yell from Polly on Mum's lap. She'd spotted a lollopy old ginger tomcat on the window sill outside. There it crouched, tapping the glass with its paw.

'It's the Mogster!' Mum screeched. 'Honestly, I swear it's stalking this baby!'

'Skedaddle, cat!' Dad shouted, rapping the window pane.

Jake and Fake Jake saw their chance. While Mum was busy comforting Polly and Dad chased away the Mogster, the spiky-haired boy (who was really a shadow) and the spiky-haired shadow (who was really a boy) made a top speed synchronized escape. They scuttled out of the kitchen, flew down the garden path and jumped nimbly over the front gate as if the two of them had never been apart in their lives.

Chapter 8
Spooking up the ghost train

When Fake Jake broke into a trot, Jake broke into a trot. When Fake Jake took a leap in the air, Jake took a leap in the air. When Fake Jake tripped over the kerb and fell flat on his face, Jake tripped over the kerb and fell flat on his face. In short, Jake was a perfect shadow.

Also, amazingly, his shadow was a perfect Jake. Was he a bit *too* perfect, Jake wondered? Suppose Fake Jake got to like being Jake so much he wouldn't go back to being a shadow? What if it was Jake who messed things up and got snuffed out by the Shadow Boss? Jake tried to shut these thoughts out of his mind.

By now, they'd reached the fun fair. The smell of yesterday's hot dogs and candyfloss hung sourly in the air. There was litter everywhere. Even the rides themselves seemed drab and worn out. But the drabbest, most worn-out ride of all was certainly the ghost train. The man in charge recognized his visitor at once.

'You're Jake, aren't you?' he snarled. 'The kid who stowed away and pretended to be a vampire!'

'I can explain,' said Fake Jake stiffly.

'Go on, then.'

'It wasn't me, you see ... '

'It wasn't you?'

'Well, it *was* me actually. But I was a shadow at the time – Jake's shadow. But now I'm not a shadow. I swapped with Jake this morning and Jake here swapped with me.'

'The two of you did *what?*'

The man's mean, knobbly face was turning red – a nasty, bullying shade of red. 'I don't care if you're a shadow, a sunbeam, or a puff of perishin' smoke,' he growled. 'Let me tell you what happened yesterday after you scared off the other passengers. Half an hour later, when they'd got over the shock, they came back for another go. They said it was the most exciting ride they'd ever had. But their next ride was useless – no vampire that time, you see. They all demanded their money back. I didn't get another customer the rest of the day – not a single blinkin' one.'

'Sorry about that – '

'Sorry's not good enough, son. What's wanted is a bit of help in spooking up this ghost train.'

'Spooking it up?'

'With bones and blood and cobwebs, for instance. Luckily, this very morning, I had a special delivery from Screams 'R' Us. All I need now is an expert to put all the new stuff in place ... a kid with vampire tendencies would do very nicely.'

'Me?' said Fake Jake, faintly.

'You,' said the man in charge of the ghost train.

Of course, it wasn't real blood or bones or
cobwebs. But if you're trapped in a dimly lit
tunnel, with only your shadow for company, they
feel every bit as creepy.

'Yikes!' Fake Jake shuddered as he tangled
himself in the spidery mush he was draping
across the track. 'Nyah!' he howled in disgust
when he caught a whiff of the crimson goo he
had to dollop over the gravestones. 'Whaaa!'
he screeched in misery after spilling a couple of
replica skeletons from the top of the ride to the
bottom in a shower of not-so-funny bones.

'It's all right for you, Jake,' Fake Jake wailed.
'While you're flitting about around me, I'm
doing all the work. Not only that – look at the
mess I'm in! You haven't got a spot on you.'

This was true. Nothing muddies a shadow.
Nothing gets stuck under a shadow's fingernails.
Nothing drips down a shadow's neck or clogs a
shadow's trainers or scrapes a shadow's knuckles.
Jake couldn't even pat his partner on the back
or give him a thumbs up. The Shadow Boss had
made that clear. A true shadow can only copy.

At last the job was finished. They waited
with bated breath while the man in charge of
the ghost train gave his verdict. 'What I'm after
here,' he told them, 'is what I call a "scare your
pants off" factor.'

'But it didn't have that before, mister!'

'What?'

'Nothing!' said Fake Jake hastily.

Luckily, his tormentor was already giving a grudging nod. 'You've done pretty well, considering,' he said. 'Of course, you owe me for all that gunge you've spilled on your kit. You weren't expecting to take it home for nothing, I hope.'

In dismay, Fake Jake stared down at his mucky clothes. 'But I haven't got any money, mister!'

'Just kidding, kid.'

To Fake Jake's relief, the man's mean, knobbly face broke into a mean, knobbly grin as he waved goodbye.

Chapter 9
Sholto's revenge

They arrived at the stables just after lunch. Miss Saddlesaw wasn't at all pleased to see them, especially when she saw the sulky look on Fake Jake's face. The ghost train had left him stained and sticky but this didn't mean he had lost his nerve. 'We're sorry, OK?' he shrugged. 'We shouldn't have dunked you in that old horse trough.'

Miss Saddlesaw glared down her horsey nose and gave a horsey, whinnying sniff. 'And who is this "we"?' she demanded.

'Me,' said Fake Jake. 'And him.'

'Him?'

Miss Saddlesaw glanced at the stable floor. There, spread bumpily over the cobblestones, Jake was copying as closely as he could. Miss Saddlesaw's eyes narrowed. 'Are you still pretending your shadow is alive, Jake?' she said icily. 'I've got the perfect cure for such nonsense!'

'What kind of cure is that?'

'Horse dung.'

'Horse dung?'

'And straw, Jake. Lots and lots of straw. There's plenty of both in Sholto's stall. By the time you've cleaned it out, mischief will be the last thing on your mind.'

'But, Miss – '

'This way, Jake.'

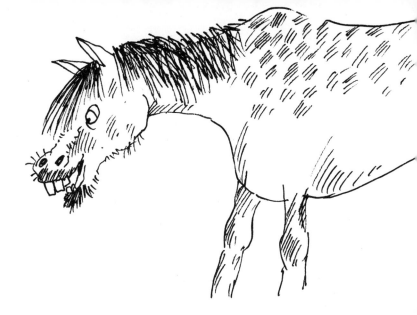

She led them straight to Sholto at the back of
the stables. 'Don't worry about disturbing my
dear old friend here,' she said. 'He's much better
behaved than some small boys I could mention.
Now, take this pitchfork and shift all the mess
into a neat, orderly stack. I'll be back in a tick
with a batch of fresh straw ready for spreading.'

'On my own?' Fake Jake protested.

'I'm sure your shadow will help if you ask
it nicely.'

Miss Saddlesaw gave a flinty smile, shut
the door of the stall behind her and strode
briskly away.

Fake Jake eyed Sholto warily. Sholto eyed Fake Jake just as warily. Or was it sleepily? Jake himself wasn't quite sure. Luckily, it wasn't his problem. Fake Jake had the problem. It's hard to scrape up straw with a pitchfork – not least when it's been thoroughly dunked in horse dung. Straw like that tends to slide through a fork's prongs and flop back on the floor. It also stirs up a bit of a stink.

'This is really gross,' said Fake Jake, holding his nose.

Finally, after a dozen false starts, Fake Jake swung his first forkful into the air ... and promptly dumped the entire load over his head and shoulders like a helping of stiff, smelly spaghetti. Sholto gave a snicker of amusement.

'I suppose you think that's funny!' Fake Jake snarled.

Sholto gave another snicker. Then Miss Saddlesaw's dear old friend tipped up a hoof and fell asleep.

Slowly, agonizingly, the pile of straw and dung grew, forkful by forkful ... with lots of slippage in between.

'I hate this job!' Fake Jake screamed. 'I've got aches and pains all over – never mind smelling like a baby's potty. This is worse than spooking up the ghost train!'

Jake kept his mouth firmly shut.

A moment later he heard the clickety-clack of Miss Saddlesaw's riding boots on the cobblestones. She was pushing an old wheelbarrow heaped with fresh, clean straw. 'How's it going, Jake?' her hoity-toity voice rang out. 'Have you finished yet?'

'Nowhere near!' Fake Jake groaned.

'I can see that,' snapped Miss Saddlesaw. 'You've hardly started, you little slacker! That's the feeblest bit of mucking out I've ever seen. There's hardly enough in the pile to fill a dustpan, let alone a wheelbarrow. Stop loafing around and get on with the job!'

With an angry toss of her plait, Miss Saddlesaw turned away. Fake Jake stood very still. Then, as rudely as he could, he stuck a thumb in either ear, poked out his tongue and waggled his fingers at her departing figure. Of course, to do this he had to let go of the pitchfork.

Luckily, Miss Saddlesaw had missed all of this. Unluckily, Sholto hadn't.

The pitchfork, you see – the heavy, unwieldy pitchfork – whacked the horse smartly across his flanks and woke him at once. Instantly, he lifted the tipped-up hoof, gave a neat little backwards kick, and flipped Fake Jake head over heels straight into the steaming mound of straw and horse dung.

'Aaagh!' came Fake Jake's strangled cry.

Miss Saddlesaw swung round in surprise. She saw what had happened at a glance. 'Naughty Sholto!' she crowed. 'Look at the mess you've made of your stall. And look at the mess you've made of Jake. You've smothered him in gunk. He'll have to start mucking out all over again, won't he – starting with himself!'

Chapter 10
Square-bashing

When Mr Snoddy opened his front door he could hardly believe his eyes. 'Why are you dressed like a scarecrow, Jake?' he barked. 'And what's that awful smell?'

'I've been spooking up a ghost train,' said Fake Jake, wearily. 'And mucking out Sholto's stall. He's Miss Saddlesaw's favourite horse ... and I don't think he likes me very much!'

'He's not the only one. Are you still sticking to your ridiculous story about your shadow running wild?'

'But it was a true story, Mr Snoddy!'

'A *true* story?'

'Every word of it. I should know, shouldn't I? It was me who fiddled with the sensors on the lawnmower and busted up your garden. You should be blaming me, not Jake.'

'Not Jake?'

'That's right.'

'But you *are* Jake!'

'No, I'm not ... Oh, I see what you mean. I forgot to tell you that we've changed places for a while.'

'You've changed places?'

'With each other, yes. This is Jake, down here, flat on the ground. And this is me – Jake's shadow – standing in front of you. It's a sort of ... a sort of experiment, I suppose.'

Mr Snoddy's face was blank. 'A sort of experiment?' he muttered. 'Is that what they call it now? Jake has turned into his shadow and his shadow has turned into Jake ...'

'You've got it, Mr Snoddy! That's really cool! You know, you're not nearly as dim as you look!'

'Aren't I, Jake?'

'Mr Snoddy?'

No wonder Fake Jake was startled. The old soldier's moustache, his eyebrows and his closely cropped hair – in fact, every bit of him that could bristle – had begun to buzz like an electric fence.

'Are you feeling OK, Mr Snoddy?' said Fake Jake in alarm.

'Silence!'

Mr Snoddy's roar was so sudden and so deafening it would have brought an entire battlefield to a halt. 'Jake,' he boomed. 'Or "Shadow", if you prefer, I think it's time we had a bit of army discipline round here. Are you familiar with the term *square-bashing*?'

'Square-bashing?'

'Drill, boy. Old-fashioned drill. It usually works a treat on the kind of youngster you are ... '

'Really?'

'Take my word for it.'

Mr Snoddy slammed the front door shut behind him. He took three crisp paces down what was left of the garden path. He threw back his shoulders, filled his chest and lifted his chin. 'Atten ... tion!' he rapped in a parade ground voice. 'Qui ... ick march!'

Fake Jake obeyed at once. After all, he knew a bit about being a soldier from movies he had watched on TV with the real Jake. What's so hard about swinging your arms, crunching your feet and going robotic for a while?

'A walk in the park, this is,' Fake Jake smirked.

And so it was ... at first.

Then the orders began to speed up: 'Right turn, left turn, about turn, change step, halt, eyes right, right dress, stand at ease, stand easy, order arms, slope arms, present arms ... '

'Hey!' Fake Jake objected. 'Can't you slow things down a bit?'

'Quiet in the ranks!' Mr Snoddy shouted.

'But Mr Snoddy – '

'Take that man's number!'

Mr Snoddy was beaming now. In his mind's eye he was a sergeant again, back at battalion HQ getting ready for a general inspection. Besides, the drill had kicked up such a cloud of dust he could hardly see his squad-of-one pounding round and round his former garden. Was it on the ninth circuit or the tenth that

he decided on a change of pace? 'Squad!' he hollered. 'Prepare for double time!'

'Double time?'

'That's when the real fun begins. With double time you repeat everything you've done at twice the speed.'

'Twice the speed?' gasped Fake Jake. 'That's impossible. I can hardly keep up at this speed!'

'Brace up, squaddie! We haven't had pack drill yet.'

'What's pack drill?'

'The same as double time, but carrying a ninety pound kitbag on your back. By the time you've mastered that, you can call yourself a proper soldier! It'll do you the world of ... Jake? Is something the matter? What are you doing down on your knees?'

'I'm feeling a bit queasy,' Fake Jake mumbled.

'A bit queasy?'

It was clear from Mr Snoddy's tone that this word didn't exist for a proper soldier. Fake Jake gave a long, lingering groan. What saved him was the tinkle of a tiny bell from inside the house.

'Well, blow me down!' said Mr Snoddy. 'Is it really four o'clock? My tea will be ready indoors. It's been a great afternoon, Jake – just like the old days. Mustn't keep my good lady waiting though or she'll put me on a charge. Shall we leave the rest of the drill till tomorrow?'

'Good idea,' croaked Fake Jake.

Chapter 11
Breaking the rules

Fake Jake was exhausted. The ghost train had spooked him. The stables had mucked him out. Mr Snoddy had square-bashed him so squarely he was almost dead on his feet. 'I feel wobbly all over,' he whimpered. 'Thank goodness our house is only next door.'

As usual, the real Jake said nothing. He didn't dare do otherwise – not while he was still flat and black and obedient, just like a proper shadow. Never in all his life had he seen such a sorry looking creature as Fake Jake.

'Talk to me, can't you?' Fake Jake begged. 'Surely you've got a shadowy tongue in your shadowy head? Why don't you chill out? You needn't do *everything* old bossy boots ordered.'

Jake didn't reply.

For him, everything old bossy boots ordered was exactly what he needed to do. A proper shadow has no choice. It sticks to the rules. If it doesn't, it knows what to expect.

Clumsily, Fake Jake pushed open the front gate. 'OK, Jake,' he sighed. 'Please yourself. I can't force a goody-goody shadow like you to speak. For once, I'm really glad to be home.'

So was Jake. The front yard wasn't up to much, really. Dad was no gardener like Mr Snoddy, but the raggedy hedge, the old wall by the washing line, and the scuffed-up lawn itself still looked golden in the afternoon sun.

'There's your little sister in her buggy,' Fake Jake pointed. 'She must be having another nap.'

Where's Mum, then? Jake almost said.

'Where's Mum, then?' Fake Jake really said. 'Has she forgotten about the Mogster?'

The Mogster?

Where was the Mogster?

Instantly, they spotted him. There he crouched, just above the buggy – three paws on the stonework and one paw reaching down – a

lollopy old ginger tomcat about to pounce on
its prey.

Jake and Fake
Jake froze. It
was the sort of
moment when
time seems to
stand still, when
the world seems to
stop spinning, when
every heart on Earth
seems to skip a beat. It
was the sort of moment
when a boy playing a shadow
could easily break the rules ...
and a shadow playing a boy could
easily be snuffed out.

Jake hurled himself forward.

So did Fake Jake.

Or was it the other way round? Not that this
mattered to the Mogster. He was grabbed by the
scruff of his neck, hoisted into the air and flung
bodily across the garden.

Naturally, he scratched a bit. He spat and yowled a bit, too, as he crash-landed on all four paws under the washing line. In one bound he shot up the garden wall, skidded over the top and pelted off to the woods in a flurry of gingery fur – just as Mum and Dad came hurrying out of the house.

'Was that the Mogster, Jake?' Dad gasped.

'Is Polly all right?' Mum yelped. 'I only left her for a second to answer the phone!'

'She's fine,' said Fake Jake.

'Really?'

'Look, Mum. She's giggling fit to burst. Maybe the Mogster only wanted to play with her.'

'Maybe he did,' said Dad, mopping his brow. 'And maybe he didn't. Either way, thank goodness you were so quick off the mark, Jake. What a wonderful big brother you are!'

'Am I?' Fake Jake said.

'The very best,' Mum added. 'For all we know, you saved Polly's life, Jake! That makes you a hero in my book!'

'A hero?'

Fake Jake blinked in surprise. It wasn't easy to feel like a hero after a day like today. Still, why argue with Jake's Mum and Dad? They'd never looked so delighted. Soon a whole bunch of shadows was spread across the garden wall in the shape of two happy grown-ups; a spiky-haired, Jake-shaped boy; and his baby sister – all kissing and cuddling each other with cries of 'What a rescue!' and 'You were just in the nick of time, Jake!' and 'Who knows what would have happened if you hadn't spotted the Mogster!'

The hugs went on and on. Nobody seemed to notice the state of the so-called hero's clothes. Or the interesting smell that came from them. Of course, they may have thought it was Polly's nappy!

Chapter 12
Medal of honour

Was it after his power shower? Or later on during Mum's special supper for the family hero? Whichever it was, somehow Jake managed to miss the exact moment when it happened. He simply realized, all of a sudden, that he was back to being himself again and his shadow was back to being a shadow – an ordinary, everyday shadow.

Life had returned to normal.

Boringly normal.

This was such a let down, Jake amazed his Mum and Dad by asking to go to bed early.

'Are you sure, Jake?' Dad asked in surprise. 'That's not like you at all. You're not getting ill, are you?'

'It's all the excitement,' said Mum. 'After a while the shock of it catches up with you.'

'That must be it, Mum,' said Jake gloomily.

Upstairs, alone in his darkened bedroom, at least he could speak to his shadow without being overheard. 'What's wrong?' he wanted to know. 'Are you in a sulk or what? I haven't heard a peep out of you for hours.'

His shadow didn't reply.

Jake shifted himself onto one elbow. 'OK, Shadow,' he said. 'Maybe you're not in the mood for talking. Why not poke out your tongue instead? Or waggle your ears? Or even pick your nose like you used to when you wanted to wind me up? At least I'd know you were still alive and kicking. If you like, you can even kick me right now.'

His shadow didn't move – not till Jake moved, anyway. Otherwise, it lay draped across his bed in the faint and rumpled outline of a spiky-haired, Jake-shaped boy.

'Last chance, Shadow,' Jake warned. 'I've got a question for you, that's all. It's really important.'

His shadow stayed silent.

Jake gritted his teeth. 'Who was it who really rescued Polly from the Mogster? Was it you or was it me? Which of us made the first move?'

His shadow still didn't answer.

Only then did the penny drop. Jake blinked at how stupid he'd been. 'It doesn't matter, does it?'

he said. 'My little sister is safe, that's all. Shall we go down and see her, Shadow?'

Out in the hallway, Jake saw that the house was already dim with evening shadows. They spilled and sloped and lurked almost everywhere he looked. Even so, he picked out his own shadow quite easily as it zig-zagged down the stairs ahead of him. 'You're copying me exactly,' said Jake. 'And we're properly linked together, just as we should be. No more tongue-poking, or ear-waggling, or nose-picking for you, matey. Your messing around days are over.'

He nodded his head to test this.

Sure enough, his shadow nodded its head as well. Nobody would guess the adventures they'd had or that, once upon a time, they'd swapped places and played at being each other. Here, just as you'd expect, was a spiky-haired, Jake-shaped boy with a spiky-haired, Jake-shaped shadow to match. There was only one small difference between them – so small, Jake had to look at it twice, sideways on, to check he'd seen it at all. Something flat and round and chunky seemed to be pinned to his shadow's chest.

'What's that you've got?' Jake asked. 'Are you wearing some kind of badge?'

Then, suddenly, he understood.

He stayed absolutely still as his shadow lifted a hand, breathed on its knuckles, and rubbed its chest in a polishing kind of way.

'Congratulations, Shadow,' Jake grinned. 'The Shadow Boss gave you your medal, after all. Is it solid gold, I wonder?'